Best of Grain Free Meal Plans Volume 1

Cara A Faus

HealthHomeHappy.com

Best of Grain Free Meal Plans Vol 1

DEDICATION

This book is dedicated to my beautiful daughter Hannah, who inspired me to start this wild grain free journey and who brings so much joy and amazement to my life.

To my handsome son Samuel, who's energy, laughter, and questions challenge me daily to try to be the best mama I can be.

And to my amazing readers, you all are on your own health journey for so many different reasons- the passion you have is contagious and I'm blessed to know you.

Best of Grain Free Meal Plans Vol 1

CONTENTS

Best of Grain Free Meal Plans Vol 1

1 BREAKFASTS

I love breakfast so much that we often eat breakfast foods for lunch and dinner as well. Grain free breakfasts push for creativity beyond cold cereal with milk, and the results are satisfying.

Beef sausage

Ingredients:
3 lbs of ground beef
1-2 onions, chopped finely
1/2 teaspoon of 3 different sweet spices (cinnamon, allspice, nutmeg, ginger etc)
1 teaspoon cayenne pepper
1 teaspoon each of at least 5 different savory spices (cumin, coriander, ground pepper, sage, oregano, etc)
2 teaspoons sea salt
1 tablespoon basil
2 eggs

Directions:
Mix all ingredients together with a fork or a stand mixer until spices are thoroughly mixed into the meat. Shape into patties and fry in coconut oil on med to med-high until no longer pink in the center. If you're pressed for time, only cook the amount you need today and form the rest into patties to stick in the freezer for later use.
If you have more time today and would like to save time later, slightly under cook all the patties and freeze. The patties will finish cooking with reheating.

Coconut Flour Banana Nut Muffins

Makes 12

1 scant cup coconut flour
3 bananas, very ripe
5 eggs
5 tablespoons butter
1 heaping teaspoon cinnamon
1/2 teaspoon salt
2 tablespoons honey (optional)
1 cup walnuts

Preheat oven to 350 degrees

Using a food processor, mix everything other than the walnuts. I used a food processor, but a mixer would work just fine too. Add in the walnuts at the end, reserving 12 to place on top if you'd like. Grease muffin pans well to prevent sticking. I used a stoneware muffin pan and greased it well with palm kernel oil; butter or coconut oil is fine to use too.

Fill muffin pans, evenly distributing the batter among all 12. Top with walnut half if desired. Bake for 25 minutes, cool a couple minutes, then remove.

Banana Pancakes

Ingredients:
6 eggs
3 extra ripe banana (yellow all over with lots of brown spots)
Butter, coconut oil, palm kernel oil, or ghee for frying.

Directions:
Heat 1 tablespoon oil or butter in a cast iron or stainless steel skillet over medium-low heat. Mash banana with a fork. Whip in eggs and combine with a fork. Use a tablespoon to spoon the batter into the oil. Flip once set, 2-3 minutes.

Berry Sauce

Ingredients:
2 cups fresh or frozen berries (blueberry, raspberry, strawberry, etc)
2 tablespoons honey

Directions:
Put berries and honey in sauce pan, cook on medium heat until berries are heated and honey is envenly distributed, approximately 10 minutes, add 2 tablespoons of water if necessary. Serve on top of pancakes or waffles.

Easy blender Hollandaise Sauce
Two fresh egg yolks
juice of one lemon
a dash of salt and pepper
1/2 cup butter - melted.

Put the egg yolk in the blender, turn it on medium, and slowly pour in the melted butter- taking maybe a minute to pour in the half cup. Then add the salt, pepper, and lemon juice. It will thicken as it cools.
I love having leftovers (we usually don't) -I use it as a spread in sandwiches the next day.

Honey Syrup:
¼ cup honey
¼ cup butter
¼ teaspoon sea salt
Melt in a small saucepan over medium heat until hot and mixed.

Coconut Flour Waffles

Makes 4 individual Belgian style waffles, or 2 large regular style. Amount will depend based on the size of your waffle maker. These are fantastic spread with dips or liver pate and used as a sandwich bread.

Ingredients:
4 Tablespoons melted coconut oil, butter, or ghee
1/4 cup coconut flour
6 eggs
2 tablespoons vanilla extract (watch for added sugar)
2 tablespoons honey
1/4 teaspoon salt

Directions:
Preheat waffle iron, grease generously with coconut oil. Mix all ingredients, allow to rest for 5 minutes so the coconut flour can absorb the liquid. Use a tablespoon to evenly distribute the batter on the iron and cook 3-4 minutes, or until golden brown.

Coconut Pancakes

Makes 12 4-inch pancakes

Ingredients:
4 eggs
1/4 cup coconut flour
1 pinch nutmeg
1 pinch cinnamon
1 tablespoon honey
1/4 cup yogurt, coconut milk, or apple sauce
Ghee, butter, or coconut oil for frying

Directions:
Mix ingredients and let them sit for five minutes. Put 1 teaspoon fat on griddle and melt over medium heat. When griddle is hot, pour 1 tablespoon of batter on for each pancake. Allow to cook until golden brown, 1-2 minutes on each side.

Troubleshooting: If your pancakes are difficult to flip, try adding an extra egg to the batter. Also, be sure to allow them to cook long enough to become golden brown before attempting to flip. Use a very thin metal spatula, not a thick plastic one.

Hootenanny Pancakes

This recipe is the closest thing I've found to sourdough bread that is grain free- we love it! The yogurt adds a bit of sourness, though coconut milk can also be used.

Ingredients:
6 eggs
1 cup yogurt
1 cup blanched almond flour
1/4 teaspoon sea salt
2 tablespoons coconut oil

Directions:
Put oil in 9" x 13" baking dish or large cast iron pan, set in oven and preheat to 425°, so the oil melts and is hot when the oven is preheated.

Beat flour, milk and eggs. When oil is melted, pour batter into it, put back in the oven and bake for 25 minutes.
Serve with fruit sauce.

Fruit Studded Scones

Ingredients:
2-1/2 cups of almond flour
1/2 teaspoons sea salt
2 eggs
4 tablespoons honey
1/4 cup softened butter, ghee, or coconut oil
1 apple, grated or ½ cup berries
1 teaspoon cinnamon

Directions:
Preheat oven to 350. Grease a baking sheet with butter or coconut oil or cover it with parchment paper.

In a medium bowl using a mixer, cream eggs, honey, and butter until light and fluffy. Mix in almond flour, sea salt, cinnamon, and apple or berries.

To shape scones, on the cookie sheet pat the dough gently into approximately an 8-inch disk. Gently cut disk into 8 wedges, like a pizza, with a large knife.

Bake 15 minutes, separate triangles, and return to oven for 10 more minutes or until done.

Scrambled Eggs with Cheese

8-10 eggs, pastured if possible
2 tablespoons butter, ghee, or coconut oil
1/2 cup cubed cheese (optional)

In a large skillet over medium heat, melt butter, ghee, or coconut oil. Tilt pan to distribute. Crack eggs into a bowl, mix gently with a fork, and pour into heated skillet. Allow the eggs to cook, stirring every 1-2 minutes. While the eggs are still runny, add cubed cheese and veggies, stir in with spatula, cook 2-3 more minutes. Remove from heat before completely cooked so the eggs do not turn dry.
Serving suggestion: Serve with cubed avocado and sliced banana.

Celeriac Hash Browns

2-3 medium celery roots
1/2 teaspoon sea salt
4 tablespoons tallow, coconut oil, or butter

Scrub and peel celery root, using a vegetable peeler or paring knife. Grate, using a cheese grater or food processor with its grating disk.

Heat a cast iron or stainless steel skillet over medium heat, melt fat in it.

Once the fat is melted, place the grated celery root in the skillet and sprinkle with salt. Sauté until it starts to get soft (about 10 minutes), then turn the heat down to medium-low and allow to cook until the hash browns are brown on the bottom (about another 10 minutes). Flip and allow the other side to brown, then serve.

Fruit smoothie

Ingredients:
1 cup fruit of your choice, frozen
1 quart kefir [page 60], yogurt [page 58] or 1 can coconut milk
2 bananas, ripe, frozen
2 tablespoons coconut oil (if not using coconut milk)
4 egg yolks from healthy chickens

Directions:
Blend coconut oil and kefir or yogurt until smooth, add remaining ingredients and blend.

Kefir Cocoa Almond Butter Smoothie

This smoothie is very filling, I'll add in nutbutters when I'm using a smoothie as a meal. The banana makes it sweet, the cocoa indulgent.

1-1/2 cups kefir [page 60]
1 frozen banana
2 tablespoons cocoa powder
2 tablespoons nut butter, preferably from nuts that have been soaked and dehydrated [page 68]

Directions: Blend until smooth.

2 LUNCH

Not being able to take the standard and ever beloved sandwich for lunch is another adjustment for the grain free foodie. The recipes that follow are new lunch ideas. Dinner leftovers are also good choices.

Toasted Sesame Chicken Stir Fry

½ cup sesame seeds (optional)
Sesame oil
2 pounds boneless chicken thighs
½ pound green beans
1 bunch green onions
1 large or 3 baby bok choy
1 cup chicken stock
¼ cup coconut milk
1 tablespoon beef gelatin (optional)
¼ teaspoon ginger
1 teaspoon sea salt
4 cloves garlic, crushed
1 lemon, juiced

Using a very sharp knife, slice raw chicken into bite sized strips and toss with 1 clove crushed garlic.

Heat a large skillet over nearly high heat. Pour sesame seeds in and, stirring continuously, toast sesame seeds for 2-3 minutes or until golden and fragrant. Set aside.

In a small saucepan, simmer chicken stock, coconut oil, salt, gelatin, and 1 clove of garlic over medium heat until reduced.

Add ½ teaspoon sesame oil to the hot skillet that the sesame seeds were toasted in, turn heat down to medium-high. Add ¼ of the chicken and cook, 10-12 minutes, stirring occasionally, until browned on the outside. Remove and cook the remaining batches of chicken.

Add more oil if necessary to the pan, and sauté the veggies in 2 batches until bright green. Combine with the remaining ingredients in a big bowl, toss, and top with toasted sesame seeds.

Almond Flour Crusted Quiche

This is a great way to use meat picked off the bones from making stock, or odds and ends of leftover meat dishes.

Crust:
Ingredients:
2 cups almond flour
2 tablespoons tallow, butter, ghee, or coconut oil
1 egg
1 teaspoon dried basil or rosemary
1/2 teaspoon sea salt

Directions:
Using a fork or mixer, mix all ingredients. Using your hands, form into a flat disk and then roll into a circle 1/4 inch thick between two pieces of parchment paper. Transfer crust to shallow casserole or pie plate. If using a pie plate. Keep the crust low and fill nearly to the top with filling to prevent the delicate almond flour from burning.

Egg Mixture for Quiche

Ingredients:
6 eggs
1/2 cup coconut milk, yogurt [page58] or cultured cream [page60]
1/2 teaspoon sea salt
1 cup cooked meat, chopped (optional)
1 bunch green onions, thinly sliced
3 leeks, rinsed and sliced into rounds

Directions:
In a bowl, combine the eggs, coconut milk, salt, and meat, mix well with a fork. Pour egg mixture into the unbaked pie crust and top with onions and leeks. Bake at 350* for 30-45 minutes, or until the center is set. Cool 15 minutes before serving to prevent quiche from crumbling.

PB&J Roll Ups

Ingredients:
Coconut flour crepes [recipe follows]
Peanut butter or other nutbutter, or dripped yogurt cheese
Blueberry Sauce [page 5]

Spread crepes 2/3 of the way up (the filling will squish) with nutbutter and blueberry syrup. Roll and secure in plastic wrap or waxed paper until lunch time.

Coconut Flour Crepes

Makes 12 crepes

Ingredients:
12 eggs
4 tablespoons coconut flour
1/8 teaspoon sea salt
6 teaspoons refined coconut oil, to fry

Directions:
Mix all ingredients well, making sure all clumps of coconut flour are broken up. Allow to sit for a few minutes.

In a skillet over medium-low heat melt 1 teaspoon of coconut oil, tilting pan to coat. Add about 2 tablespoons of batter and tilt to make a 6-inch circle. Cook until bubbles start to form and the middle of the pancake looks slightly cooked. Flip gently with a thin spatula and cook until the other side is golden; about 5 minutes on the first side, 2 on the second.

Guacamole Burgers

I find grassfed beef to be so tasty on its own that I only season my hamburgers with a little sea salt and freshly ground pepper.

Ingredients:
2 pounds grassfed organic ground beef, full fat
1/2 teaspoon sea salt
1/2 teaspoon freshly ground pepper

Directions:
Preheat a cast iron skillet over medium-high heat.
Mix meat, salt, and pepper with a fork. Form into 6 patties with hands.
Cook on medium-high heat until the bottom is nicely browned, flip, and then turn down to medium to cook the rest of the way through - approxamately 10 minutes on the first side and 5 on the second.

Top with guacamole [page 18], cheese, sliced onions, and tomato.

Guacamole

Ingredients:
2-3 ripe avocados
2 cloves garlic, pressed
1 teaspoon cumin
1/2 teaspoon sea salt
Juice of one lemon

Directions:
Slice avocados lengthwise all the way around, down to the pit. Twist to separate halves. Remove pit with knife and scoop out avocado with a spoon.

Mash in 2-3 ripe avocados with a fork. Add remaining ingredients and mix well. If storing, press plastic wrap right up against the guacamole to help prevent it from oxidizing and turning brown, store in the fridge for a couple hours.

Butternut Squash Pizza

Ingredients:
1 large butternut squash
1 cup spicy sausage, crumbled and browned [page 2]
1 large tomato, thinly sliced
1 cup Monterey jack cheese, shredded (optional)
Coconut oil for the pan

Directions:
Preheat oven to 400°.
Using a vegetable peeler, peel the neck of the butternut squash, slice into 1/2 inch thick rounds.
Grease the bottom of two 9x13 inch pans or a large cookie sheet with coconut oil. Lay squash in a single layer along bottom. Bake for 15 minutes, flip, and top with tomato, sausage and cheese. Return to the oven for another 15 minutes.

These are easiest to eat with a fork. Enjoy!

'Meal' Salad
Meal salads are wonderful for spring and summer. Crunchy greens with lots of toppings.

Ingredients:
1 pound greens; spinach, lettuce, cabbage
2 tomatoes, chopped
1 onion, diced
1/2 cup black olives
1 cup shredded cheese (optional)
1 cup crispy nuts, chopped
1/2 cup sunflower seeds
1 pound cooked boneless chicken, or leftover fried chicken, sliced

Directions:
Layer all ingredients and toss with dressing right before serving

Summer Coconut Dressing

Ingredients:
Juice of 4 limes
2 teaspoons almond butter or tahini
1/4 cup coconut milk
3 sprigs of cilantro, finely chopped
3 sprigs fresh mint, finely chopped
1/8 teaspoon cayenne pepper (optional)
1/4 teaspoon sea salt

Directions:
Mix all ingredients. Store any extra covered in the fridge.

3 DINNER

Grain free dinners can be dressed up or simple, but are always satisfying with lots of protein rich meat and colorful veggies.

Baked Fried Chicken
This simple crunchy chicken can easily be made ahead of time, which means less hands on time for you during the dinner rush!

Ingredients:
3 pounds boneless chicken
3/4 cup almond flour or almond meal
1/2 teaspoon salt
1/4 teaspoon black pepper
1 teaspoon Italian seasoning, or a mix of basil, parsley, and oregano
1/8 teaspoon cayenne pepper (optional)
1 tablespoon oil, tallow, or butter for greasing pan

Directions:
Grease two 9x13" pans, or a large cookie sheet with sides (to contain juices) with fat. Combine almond flour, salt, pepper, and seasonings in a shallow bowl. Rinse chicken and dip into almond flour mixture, pressing into the mixture on all sides so that it is covered. Lay chicken on cookie sheet. Repeat with remaining chicken pieces, placing them in a single layer, touching is okay. Bake at 375* for 35 minutes, or until chicken is cooked through.

Burrito Bowl

2 pounds ground beef, browned
For the beef: {1/2 teaspoon sea salt, 1 teaspoon smoked paprika, 1 pinch
cayenne, 1/2 teaspoon ground cumin}
1 pound navy beans
2 quarts chicken stock [page 66]
Filtered water
4 tomatoes, chopped
1 onion, diced
1 bunch fresh parsley, diced
1-2 cups grated cheese
1-2 cups yogurt or cultured cream- as sour cream
Guacamole [page 18]
1 head lettuce

Soak beans to make them more easily digestible: Rinse one pound (2 cups) of
navy beans in a colander, removing any rocks or debris that may be mixed in.
Put in a large bowl (they will swell to triple their current size) and cover with
filtered water so that they are covered by an inch or more. Allow to soak for
24 hours, changing the water once during this time.

Cook soaked beans in crock pot overnight or all day on low with 2 quarts
chicken stock and 2 quarts of water, adding a pinch of baking soda if they do
not get soft.
[continued on page 24]

[Burrito Bowl Continued]

Season beef and start browning in a cast iron or stainless steel skillet over medium-high heat, breaking up the beef as it cooks.

As the beef browns, chop the tomatoes, onions, and parsley and toss together. Grate the cheese. Make guacamole.

Wash and tear lettuce, place in bowls.

Top lettuce with beans, meat, tomato mixture, cheese, guacamole, and sour cream. Each person can adjust the toppings as they desire.

Salmon Patties

This fast meal is nutrient dense, loved by children, and takes less time to make than boxed macaroni and cheese! Serve with some frozen peas or cultured vegetables for a complete meal. Shown here with Easy Blender Hollandaise Sauce [page 5]

Ingredients:
2 6-ounce cans wild caught salmon
2 eggs
¼ cup shredded coconut to hold together
¼ cup coconut oil to fry.

Directions:
    Preheat oil to medium-high heat. Combine the rest of the ingredients in a small bowl. Form into patties with your hands, packing firmly. Fry in palm kernel oil or coconut oil on medium-high heat. Flip once browned, about 5 minutes on each side.

Chicken Pepper Poppers

Serves 6-8

Ingredients:
2 pounds boneless chicken
4 Anaheim chilies
1 pound bacon
1 pound baby tomatoes (optional)
Wooden Skewers

Directions:
Freeze the chicken for 20 minutes (set a timer so you don't forget!) so it is easier to cut. Cut into bite-sized pieces.

Wash the chilies, cut the stem off, and cut a slit down the side. Use your finger, under running water, to remove seeds. Cut chilies into 2-inch long segments.

Preheat oven to 425°.

Stuff a bite sized piece of chicken into a pepper piece, then wrap a piece of bacon tightly around pepper, stick the whole roll up on a wooden skewer. If your bacon is long enough, you may wish to cut it in half, so it only wraps around the pepper once.

Push the roll up all the way to the end and then continue with the chicken/pepper/bacon wraps, spacing them about 1/8 – 1/4 inch apart on the skewer, 6 to a skewer.

If desired, space with baby tomatoes.

Bake for 25 minutes, or until chicken is cooked through.

You can cut skewers in half (using wire cutters is easiest) after cooking. This is perfect for potlucks and feeding children when 'just a taste' is desired.

Butternut Squash and Beef Casserole

Alternatively you can top the butternut squash with extra beef sausage meat (raw) from page 2.

Serves 4

Ingredients:
2 pounds hamburger
1 large butternut squash (3 pounds)
1 teaspoon sea salt
2 cups stock
Tallow or fat to grease pan

Directions:
Preheat oven to 350°. Mix hamburger with sea salt. Peel and remove pulp from butternut squash, chop into 1" cubes. Grease a 9x13" pan with fat. Place squash in the pan and pour stock over the squash. Place pieces of the raw hamburger over the top of the squash, covering evenly. Bake uncovered for 45 minutes or until squash is soft and beef is cooked.

Lamb Roast

Serves 4 with enough for leftovers for another meal

Ingredients:
1 boneless lamb roast, 3-4 lbs
8 cloves garlic, peeled and sliced into slivers
1 tablespoon coarse salt
1 tablespoon olive oil

Directions:
Remove lamb from packaging. If it is in a net, keep the netting on. If not, secure with kitchen twine by rolling the lamb into a log, and wrapping the twine around the roast every 1-2 inches and tying. Place the lamb on a baking dish and preheat oven to 400°. Using a paring or steak knife, make slits every 3-4 inches across the top of the lamb in a loose grid about 1 inch deep. Insert a sliver of garlic into each slice, pushing the garlic as far in as you can. Sprinkle the roast with coarse salt and drizzle with olive oil. Bake until an internal temperature reaches 140*, checking at 45 minutes and periodically thereafter. Remove from oven and allow to rest for at least 30 minutes, lamb will continue to rise in temperature as it rests. After resting, remove netting or twine and slice to serve.

Sushi made with Celery Root 'Rice'

Lemon Juice 'Cooked' Fish
Ingredients:
1/4 pound Ahi Tuna Steak, wild caught
1/4 pound Cod, wild caught
Juice of 2 lemons
Juice of 2 limes
Directions:
Pick out any bones and cut fish into bite sized pieces. Place in a bowl and cover with lemon and lime juice. Cover and refrigerate overnight or 2-3 hours, or until somewhat firm and no longer transparent. Drain juice.

Grain Free Sushi Rice
Ingredients:
1-2 medium celery roots, (to make approx 6 cups shredded)
2 tablespoons honey
2 tablespoons apple cider vinegar
1 teaspoon coarse sea salt

Directions:
Peel celery root and shred, using a

grater or the grater attachment on a food processor. Toss shredded celery root in honey, sea salt, and apple cider vinegar.

Sushi Filling

Ingredients:
Fish, as described above
carrots, cut into matchsticks
mango, cut into thin slices
Avocado, sliced
Green onions, just the white and light green parts, thinly sliced
Cucumbers, cultured or fresh, thinly sliced
Pickled Ginger
Nori Sheets

Directions:
To fill the sushi, lay out a square nori sheet Press 1/2 cup of rice mixture onto the bottom half of the nori sheet. Spread desired fillings down the center of the rice. Use mat to roll up sushi roll firmly, moisten end of nori sheet to hold together. Slice with a sharp knife and enjoy!

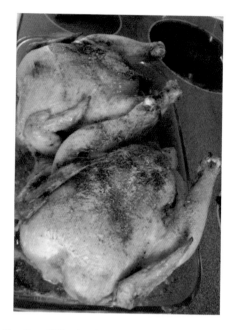

Roasted or Slow Cooker Whole Chicken

1 whole chicken
Crockpot
Optional seasonings, a pinch of any or all: Sea salt, ground pepper, paprika, chili powder, thyme, ground ginger

Directions:
Remove chicken from packaging. Reach inside cavity and remove giblet package.
Crockpot: Place chicken in slow cooker, sprinkle with desired seasoning. Cover, and turn on low overnight. In the morning turn off, and allow to cool.
Oven Roast: Alternatively, sprinkle with seasoning and bake uncovered at 375* for 1-1/2 hours or until juices run clear when drumstick is cut into with a sharp knife.

Hearty Red Chili

Ingredients:
2 pounds ground beef
1 pound beef liver, chopped into tiny pieces
4 onions, chopped
1 cup finely chopped fresh cilantro (optional)
3 tablespoons ground cumin
3 tablespoons chili powder
3 cloves garlic, crushed
2 1/2 cups (or more) stock

1 can tomato paste or 1 1/2 cups diced tomatoes
1 tablespoon sea salt
1 tablespoon honey

Toppings:
Grated or crumbled cheddar cheese
Yogurt (as sour cream)
Additional chopped onion

Directions:
Soak Liver: *Liver is soaked the day before to remove excess blood and prevent bitterness. Chicken or lamb liver can also be used.*
Drain any blood from thawed liver. Place in a bowl. Cover with the juice of one lemon and filtered water until the liver is completely covered. Cover bowl with lid or plastic wrap and return to the fridge.
Chili:
Sauté beef, liver and 2 cups chopped onions in large Dutch oven over medium heat until beef is cooked through, stirring often

and breaking up beef with back of spoon, about 10 minutes. Add cumin, chili powder, garlic powder and chipotle chilies; sauté 3 minutes. Mix in 2 1/2 cups stock and 1/2 cup cilantro. Reduce heat to medium-low. Cover partially and cook 1 1/2 hours, adding more water by 1/4 cupfuls if chili becomes dry. Season with salt and pepper. (Can be made 1 day ahead. Cover; chill. Bring to simmer before continuing.)
Mix remaining 1/2 cup cilantro into chili. Ladle chili into bowls. Serve, top with toppings individually as desired.

White Bean Chili

Ingredients:
2 tablespoons butter or ghee
1 whole medium onion, diced
4 cloves garlic, crushed
2 Anaheim chilis, seeds removed, diced
1 lb Navy Beans
4 cups chicken broth
4 cups filtered water
1 whole Jalapeno, Sliced
1 tablespoon Ground Cumin
1 teaspoon paprika
1/2 teaspoon cayenne pepper
Sea Salt to taste (start with 1 tablespoon)
1 cup yogurt
2 egg yolks
3 Cups cooked chicken diced
8 ounces grated Monterey Jack cheese

Top with:
Yogurt
Guacamole (optional)

Directions:
Soak beans:
Rinse one pound (2 cups) of navy beans in a colander, removing any rocks or debris that may be in the package. Put in a large bowl (they will swell to triple their current size) and cover with filtered water so that they are covered by an inch or more. Allow to soak for 24 hours, changing the water once during this timeperiod.
Cook soaked beans in crock pot overnight on low with 2 quarts chicken stock and 2 quarts of water, adding a pinch of baking soda if they do not get soft.

In a skillet over medium heat cook the onion and garlic in butter until soft. Transfer to crockpot, add the rest of the ingredients except yogurt, yolks and cheese. Cook in the crock pot all day on low, or 4 hours on high. 20 minutes before serving mix together egg yolks and yogurt and add to chili. Once the yogurt mixture is stirred in, add the cheese and stir to melt.

4 SOUPS

Soups are a warming comfort food full of veggies and nourishing broth. Starting them in the crock pot in the morning makes the house so welcoming to come home to at night.

Butternut Squash Soup

The fragrant additions of garlic and ginger also make this a great soup for when viruses are going around.

Ingredients:
2-3 lbs butternut squash, peeled and chopped
1 quart chicken stock [page 66]
2 tablespoons sea salt
4 cloves garlic
1 inch peeled ginger root
Filtered water

Directions:
Peel butternut squash, discard pulp, and chop flesh into 2-3 inch chunks. Place in crock pot and add 1 quart of chicken broth, fill to within 3 inches of the top with filtered water. Add 2 tablespoons sea salt, 4 cloves of crushed garlic, 1 inch of peeled ginger root finely diced. Cover, and allow to cook on low all day. Puree with immersion blender and serve topped with cultured cream [page 60]

Cold Beet Soup

This deep red soup is a fun change. Cold soup is also an easy 'fast food' that is low sugar and rich in amino acids from the chicken stock.

4 medium beets, peeled and chopped
4 carrots, peeled and chopped
3 cups stock, or more to thin the soup as desired [page 66]
½ teaspoon sea salt, or to taste
¼ teaspoon pepper
¼ teaspoon cayenne pepper (optional)
¼ cup fresh dill, finely chopped (optional)
2 cloves garlic (add more to taste)

Cultured cream, to serve (optional) [page 60]

Directions:
Place the beets, carrots, and stock in a crock pot. Cook on low 8 hours or high 4 hours, until the beets are soft. Add remaining ingredients and puree in a food processor or with an immersion blender. Add more stock to thin if necessary. Chill well and serve topped with yogurt or cultured cream as desired.

Onion Soup

Caramelizing the onions for onion soup does take a bit of time, but it isn't all hands on time and it adds an amazing depth to the finished soup.

Ingredients:
4 large onions, sliced into approximately 1/4 inch rounds
2 tablespoons butter, ghee, or chicken fat
1 quart chicken stock [page 66]
filtered water
1-2 tablespoons sea salt

Directions:
In a saucepan, melt butter over medium-low heat. Add onions and allow onions to cook uncovered, stirring every 5-10 minutes, until they turn a golden brown, approximately 30 minutes. Remove from heat.

In a crock pot add caramelized onions, chicken stock, sea salt (start with less and add salt to taste before serving). Add 2-3 quarts of filtered water, or as much needed to fill the crock pot at least 2/3 full.

Turn on low and allow to cook all day, or high and allow to heat 2-3 hours or until heated through. Enjoy garnished with grated parmesan cheese.

Roasted Carrot Soup

Carrots are inexpensive, which can be helpful when eating grain free. Roasting them adds a fantastic flavor.

Ingredients:
5-6 large organic carrots, scrubbed
2 large onions, peeled and quartered
6 cloves garlic, peeled
2 cups pumpkin chunks (peeled, without the pump) or 1 cup pumpkin puree [page 70]
2 tablespoons butter, ghee, or tallow
1 tablespoon paprika
1 teaspoon sea salt
1 quart chicken stock [page 66]
2 quarts filtered water
1-2 tablespoons sea salt, to taste

Directions:
Cut carrots into 3-4 inch pieces. In an oven-safe dish pile all the vegetables, garlic, and pumpkin. Dot across the top with fat, and sprinkle with paprika and sea salt.

Place in the oven to roast at 300° for an hour. No need to preheat.

In a crock pot, place the roasted vegetables and drain the juices and melted fat from the bottom of the pan into the crockpot as well. Add chicken stock and enough filtered water to cover the vegetables. Cook on low all day, or high for 4 hours.

Spoon into bowls and garnish with grated parmesan cheese, cultured cream, and/or paprika.

5 SNACKS AND SIDES

Snacks that can be eaten on the run and side dishes that don't feature grains and starches are the two areas that usually take the most adjustment when enjoying a grain free diet. Here are plenty of tasty ideas to get you through!

Butternut Squash Chips

The crunch and saltiness of chips, without the mess and expense of deep frying.

Ingredients:
2 large butternut squash necks
2 tablespoons olive oil
1/4 teaspoon sea salt

Directions:
Peel butternut squash neck (reserve the bulb portion for another use such as butternut squash soup on page 34)
Slice as thinly as possible into rounds
Toss with olive oil in a bowl, using your hands or a fork if you wish
Lay in a single layer on dehydrator tray, sprinkle with salt.
Dehydrate 12 hours, or until crisp, on high if your dehydrator has temperature settings.
Enjoy!

Pea Salad

This simple salad is child friendly and a change of pace from leafy greens

1 pound frozen peas, thawed or fresh peas, blanched
1/4 cup radishes, diced
1/2 onion, diced (optional)
1/4 cup mayonnaise [page 67]
2 sprigs of mint, diced
1/2 teaspoon sea salt
2 tablespoons apple cider vinegar

Mix all ingredients, chill before serving. Tip: Pull the peas out to thaw in the morning, drain any water that may have been released, then add in remaining ingredients.

Garlic Sautéed Asparagus

1 pound asparagus, rinsed
2 cloves garlic, crushed
½ teaspoon sea salt
1 tablespoon butter or animal fat

In a skillet, heat fat over medium heat. Add in garlic. Meanwhile, cut and discard the bottom inch off of the asparagus spears, and cut into 1-inch pieces. Add asparagus pieces to hot fat and garlic, sprinkle with salt, and allow to cook, stirring every minute to prevent sticking. Cook for 10 minutes or until slightly soft and bright green. Serve warm or room temperature.

Garlic-Spinach Artichoke Dip

1/3 cup mayonnaise
2 cups fresh spinach
2 cloves garlic

Puree above ingredients in food processor, add in

½ cup artichoke hearts

Pulse to chop

2 cups Parmesan, grated

Pulse to mix in the cheese and enjoy! Keep covered in the refrigerator if you have leftovers. Leftovers can be used as sandwich spreads and to stuff peppers with (bake at 375* on the top rack for 20 minutes or until hot and bubbly).

Slow Cooker Apple Sauce

This fresh apple sauce makes good use of apples for sale at harvest from local farm stands. The peel is left on for added nutrition.

Ingredients:

8-12 medium-sized apples or a combination of apples and ripe pears
½ cup honey (optional)
½ cup water
1 tablespoon cinnamon

Instructions:

Rinse apples, core, and slice. Don't peel. Put in slow cooker along with honey, water, and cinnamon and turn on low 12 hours or over night. Puree in the crockpot with an immersion blender, or transfer to a food processor or blender and puree. Spoon into jars and keep in the refrigerator or freezer.

Deviled eggs

Ingredients:
6 eggs, hard boiled
3-4 tablespoons homemade mayonnaise
1 teaspoon prepared mustard or 1/4 teaspoon mustard powder
1/2 teaspoon sea salt

Paprika for garnish

Hard Boiled Egg Instructions
6 eggs
Filtered water
½ teaspoon olive or coconut oil
½ teaspoon sea salt.

Fill a large pot half full of filtered water and bring to a boil. Add oil and sea salt; the oil makes the shells easier to peel off, the sea salt helps prevent the white from leaking should the eggs become cracked while boiling. Gently put whole raw eggs in the water, using a slotted spoon if needed to prevent them from cracking.

Boil eggs on medium-high heat for exactly 10 minutes. After 10 minutes pour off excess boiling water and add cold water to the eggs to cool. As the water heats, replace with cold water 2-3 times; every couple minutes. Store eggs in the fridge or peel immediately.

Gently peel eggs under running water. Slice in half lengthwise. Pop yolks into a sandwich-sized zip top bag (or a bowl). Add remaining ingredients and smash with your fingers in the zip top bag (or smash with a fork in the bowl). Add more mayonnaise if necessary. Once thoroughly mixed, cut a corner off the bottom of the zip top bag, approximately 1/2 inch up from the top of the corner. Pipe the yolk mixture into the egg whites, or use a spoon to drop the mixture into the egg whites, and then garnish with paprika.

Keep covered in the fridge if you have leftovers.

www.healthhomehappy.com

Fried Cheese Sticks

Everyone's favorite recipe! If you are dairy free, you can use cauliflower or other fast-cooking vegetables in place of the cheese. Omit the freezing step.

Ingredients:
12 Monterey Jack cheese sticks
4 eggs
1 cup blanched almond flour
1 tablespoon Italian Seasoning
2 cups expeller pressed coconut oil

Directions:
A few hours or more before cooking put cheese sticks in the freezer. You can cut your own sticks from a large block of cheese, or purchase pre-wrapped cheese sticks. When ready to make the fried cheese sticks, heat the oil over medium heat in as small of a sauce pan as you can fit the cheese sticks in. Using a small pan allows the oil to be deeper.

In a shallow bowl or dish mix almond flour with Italian Seasoning.

Lightly beat eggs in another shallow dish.

Take frozen cheese sticks out and dip 1 to 3 at a time in the egg, allow egg to drip off, and then roll in the almond flour mixture until well covered. Drop into the hot oil and fry for 1-2 minutes, or until golden brown. The cheese sticks will likely float to the top of the oil at this time. Remove from oil and drain on a plate.

Serve with homemade ranch dressing, red sauce, or barbeque sauce.

Onion Muffins

Ingredients:
6 eggs
2 small onions
1/2 cup cheese 'chunks' (optional)
1/4 cup coconut flour
1/2 teaspoon salt

Directions:
Preheat oven to 375*
Using a blender or food processor, puree onions. Add in coconut flour, eggs, and salt. Puree until coconut flour is well mixed in, then stir in optional cheese chunks.
Grease a muffin pan or put in muffin liners. Fill the cups 1/2 full with batter, it should make 12. Bake for 17-20 minutes or until a knife inserted comes out clean. Allow to cool slightly before removing.

www.healthhomehappy.com

Sesame Sunflower Seed Crackers

Ingredients:
1 cup unsalted sunflower seeds, hulled
1 teaspoon sea salt (the coarse kind is fine)
3 cloves of garlic, peeled
1 cup sesame seeds, hulled
Up to 1/4 cup water

Directions:
Preheat oven to 375°.
In the bowl of the food processor, using the regular metal blade, combine the sunflower seeds, salt, and garlic. Turn food processor on and let it whir for 2-3 minutes until the seeds have turned into a dense flour. Add in the sesame seeds and pulse to mix (the sesame seeds don't need to mix all the way in). Slowly add in the water, a couple tablespoons at a time, until the seeds all clump together in a ball. Remove and knead to distribute the sesame seeds through the sunflower seed mixture. The mixture isn't a very pretty color at this point, but it improves beautifully with baking.

Between parchment paper, roll the dough out until it is 1/4 thick, in as close to a rectangle shape as possible. Slide the parchment paper with rolled out cracker dough onto a baking sheet. Remove top parchment paper. Cut into rectangles into dough with a pizza cutter or sharp knife.
Bake for 15-20 minutes, or until golden brown. Allow to cool while still on the cookie sheet, then break along scored lines and serve. Store in airtight container.

6 DESSERT

Who doesn't love a sweet ending to a meal? And when serving guests who may not be as into healthy eating as you are, a wholesome tasty treat goes a long way to convincing them that you don't really live a life of deprivation, but grain free can actually taste quite good!

Chocolate Truffles

Makes approximately 40 truffles

1 cup cocoa powder
1/4 cup coconut oil, melted
1/4 cup honey
1/2 cup coconut cream (the cream from the top of a full fat unsweetened can of coconut)

Directions:
(These are amazingly simple!) Mix all ingredients in a small mixing bowl with a fork, making sure to mix bottom and sides in well. Cover and place in the freezer for 15-20 minutes or until firm. Pour a little more cocoa, or shredded coconut or chopped nuts, into a shallow bowl (about 2 tablespoons) for the coating.
Scoop out a small spoonful of the hardened chocolate, gently roll it in your hands, and drop it in the bowl with coating. Once you have a couple you can gently swirl the bowl to cover the ball with the cocoa powder. This was the part my toddler got a kick out of. Then place the covered truffles on a plate and repeat with the remaining chocolate.

Orange Vanilla Grain Free Cupcakes

Makes 1 dozen cupcakes

6 eggs
1/4 cup coconut oil, butter, or ghee
1/4 cup coconut milk
1/8 cup honey
1/2 teaspoon orange zest
1 tablespoon orange juice concentrate (optional)
1 tablespoon vanilla extract
1/2 cup coconut flour
1/2 teaspoon sea salt

Instructions

Preheat oven to 350 degrees. Grease muffin tray with coconut oil or use cupcake liners. If using cupcake liners, drop approximately 1/4 teaspoon coconut oil in the bottom of each liner and place in the oven while combining ingredients- the oil will wick up the liner to grease it, a healthier alternative to pressurized baking sprays.

In a food processor, blender, or in a bowl with a whisk, combine all ingredients, using a spatula to scrape the sides of the bowl to make sure the coconut flour is mixed in well.

Bake cupcakes for 25 minutes or until a toothpick inserted into the center of one comes out clean. These freeze well, frosted or unfrosted.

Simple Meringue Frosting Recipe

This recipe takes less than 10 minutes, but it does have to be done all at once. The honey must be poured into the egg whites while it is still hot or it will solidify. The hot honey also cooks the egg whites. This does make quite a bit, enough to frost 2 dozen cupcakes.

Ingredients:
1/2 cup honey
2 egg whites, (eggs at room temperature)
1/4 teaspoon sea salt
1/2 teaspoon vanilla (optional)

Directions:
Heat honey in a saucepan over medium heat 5-10 minutes; until mixture bubbles and darkens.
Meanwhile, separate two eggs, being very careful to avoid getting any yolk in with the whites.
Add the salt to the egg whites.
Put two whites in a stand mixer with a whip attachment, or use a hand held mixer and a bowl held steady by a helper.
Mix starting on medium.
As the eggs start to froth, turn the mixer up to high.
At the same time you turn the mixer up to high, start pouring the honey in with a thin steady stream, taking about 1 minute to pour in the hot honey.
Continue mixing on high as the frosting fluffs and thickens and is cool enough to touch, 2-3 minutes.
Add the optional vanilla while mixing.
Use a spatula or butter knife to frost cupcakes, or spoon into a piping bag and pipe onto cupcakes for a more decorative look. The icing goes on the cupcakes or cake easiest if used within a couple hours of making.

Slow Cooker Baked Apples

These are great for dessert or breakfast, mmm, make the house smell so good!

Ingredients:
6 medium to large green apples
1/4 cup raisins
1/4 cup honey
1 teaspoon cinnamon
6 tablespoons coconut oil, butter, or ghee

Directions:
Core apples. To core, using an apple corer or paring knife, cut around the core (about 1/2 inch from the stem all the way around) but leave about half an inch at the bottom. Use the knife to 'drill out' the core. Divide raisins, honey, cinnamon, and coconut oil between the apples. Place apples in a crock pot and add 1/2 inch of water. Cook on low overnight and enjoy a hot breakfast in the morning!
Alternatively, bake covered at 350 degrees in a glass dish for 45 minutes-1 hour in the morning.
Top with cream, yogurt, coconut milk, or just eat plain.

Butter Cookies
Makes 24 cookies

2 1/2 cups blanched almond flour
1/2 teaspoon sea salt
1/2 cup salted butter, cut into pieces
Scant 1/4 cup honey
1 teaspoon cinnamon

In a food processor, place almond flour and salt and pulse briefly
Add butter, honey and cinnamon and pulse until ingredients are well
blended. Use your hands to roll dough into small balls and flatten with the
bottom of a glass on a parchment paper lined cookie sheet until ¼ inch thick.
Bake at 350° for 5-7 minutes
Cool and serve.

Chocolate Peanutbutter Cookies
Makes 2 dozen

Ingredients:
1 cup natural peanut or almond butter, salt added (add 1/2 teaspoon salt if unsalted)
1/4 cup coconut oil
2 tablespoons coconut flour
1/4 cup honey
4 eggs
1/4 cup unsweetened cocoa

Directions:
Combine all ingredients until thoroughly mixed. Use a teaspoon to spoon dough onto parchment lined cookie sheet. To make cris-cross decorations with a fork, dip fork prongs in water, and press into cookies, twice, 90 degrees apart. Bake at 375° for 10-12 minutes, do not over bake.

Cowboy Cookies
Makes 2-3 dozen

Ingredients:
2 1/2 cups almond flour
2 tablespoons coconut flour
1/2 teaspoon sea salt
1/2 cup coconut oil or butter
2 eggs
1 tablespoon vanilla extract
1/2 cup honey
1/2 cup chopped pecans
1/4 cup shredded coconut
1/4 cup raisins or other dried fruit, chopped

Directions:
Cream oil, honey, and coconut oil or butter. Add in remaining ingredients and mix well
Drop teaspoonfulls about 2 inches apart on a parchment lined baking sheet
Bake at 350 degrees for 7-10 minutes.
Cool and serve.

Slow Cooker Butternut Custard

Ingredients:
2 cups cooked winter squash [page 70], or canned pumpkin
6 egg yolks + 3 whole eggs (or 8 whole eggs)
1 or 2 tablespoons honey
dash of sea salt
1/2 cup cultured cream [page 60] or coconut milk
1 tablespoon unflavored gelatin (optional)

Directions:
Thoroughly mix, place in a greased pie dish or individual custard cups. Fill a large
Bake at 350 for 40 minutes.

Crockpot Instructions: Fill crockpot with 2 inches of water. Turn on high for 1 hour.
Add custard cups, stacking if necessary. Cook in crockpot for 3-4 hours or until
cooked through- this makes the house smell amazing, so nice to come home to on a
cool fall or winter afternoon.

7 CULTURED FOODS

Cultured foods are not only a great way to preserve fresh veggies, and dairy, but supply the body with beneficial microorganisms needed for health. If you haven't cultured your own foods before, I would encourage you to try it- turning your kitchen into a mini biology lab is fun and makes you feel quite accomplished (and a little rebellious!).

24-hour SCD Yogurt

The 24-hour incubation at 100 degrees F gives the culture sufficient time to use up the vast majority of the lactose, making yogurt acceptable low/no lactose diets.

Ingredients:
1/2 gallon milk (goat or cow, raw or pasteurized)
Yogurt starter, either a packet (follow instructions) or high quality store bought yogurt with active cultures, 1 tablespoon per quart.

Directions:
In a stock pot, heat milk gently on medium heat, stirring approximately every 10 minutes, until milk is close to a boil. About 190°.
Cover, remove from burner, and allow to cool until the yogurt is comfortable to the touch, 90-110* F.
Make sure the yogurt is not too hot at this stage, or you will kill the good bacteria that is going to make your milk into yogurt.
Pour barely warm milk into jars, quarts are a good size.
Using one tablespoon of commercial yogurt per quart, (or follow the directions that came with your powdered starter) mix yogurt or starter into the jars of warm milk.
Cover, and shake to distribute culture.
Keep warm in a yogurt maker, Excalibur dehydrator, or insulated cooler at 100 degrees for a full 24 hours. Yogurt is now done and should be kept in the refrigerator.

Dripped yogurt 'cream cheese' and whey

Ingredients:
2 cups yogurt [page 58]

Equipment:
1 coffee filter, double layer of cheese cloth, or thin very clean dish towel
Sieve
Bowl that the sieve can easily rest over without touching the bottom.

Directions:
Put the sieve into the bowl, then the coffee filter, clean cloth, or cheesecloth in the sieve. Pour in 2 cups of yogurt. Cover with plastic wrap and place in the fridge all day or overnight. What remains is yogurt cheese, transfer cheese to a sealed container and use within a couple days. What dripped out is whey, reserve this in a mason jar with a lid for a month or two, it is added to ferments to increase probiotic activity.

Homemade Kefir

Kefir is cultured dairy like yogurt is, but it remains more liquid, and it contains different cultures than yogurt does.

Ingredients:
1 quart milk, cream, or combination of milk and cream (optional: 1 quart nondairy milk + 1/4 cup honey)
1 tablespoon kefir grains, milk kefir grains for dairy, water kefir grains for nondairy kefir.

Directions:
In a quart jar, place milk, sweetener if needed, and kefir grains. Allow to ferment covered 24 hours, strain out grains, and store grains (covered with liquid) and kefir in the fridge, covered.

Lacto-Fermented Dilly Carrot Sticks

These are great foods for little ones to snack on, they are a bit softer than plain carrot sticks, and have all the benefits of cultured vegetables.

Ingredients:
6 medium carrots, peeled and cut into sticks
1 tablespoon whey (optional) [page 59]
1 tablespoon sea salt
1 tablespoon chopped fresh dill, or 1 teaspoon dried
3 cloves of garlic, quartered (optional)
Filtered water

Directions:
Place the carrot sticks into a quart mason jar (or other quart sized container with a lid that fits snugly) and add the rest of the ingredients, shaking gently to settle the carrots if needed.
Fill to within one inch of the top with filtered water.
Cover tightly and allow to sit at room temperature for 4-7 days; you can try them at 4 days and see if you want them to be more sour or not, to get them more sour/soft leave them out at room temperature longer. Because the carrots are more dense, they take longer to ferment than other lactoferments like sauerkraut or pickles. They also stay crunchier.
After fermenting at room temperature, keep in your fridge- they last for months!

Kimchi
Makes 4 pint jars full.

Ingredients:
1 napa cabbage
1 bunch of green onions
3 carrots
1 bunch of radishes
1 tablespoon fresh ginger, grated
4 cloves of garlic
4 chili peppers (mild or spicy, depending on your taste preference)
4 teaspoons sea salt
1 teaspoon whey per mason jar (optional) [page 59]

Directions:
Aside from the ginger and carrots, which you might want to grate smaller, thinly slice all the vegetables and mix with the salt. Place into jars, pounding down to release juice. Add whey over the top, cover with a lid, and set in a room temperature place to ferment for 2-3 days without opening. Transfer to fridge after that and enjoy now or later. Left unopened, my ferments last months in my fridge, but once you open them, use within a couple weeks.

Sauerkraut

The kraut pictured is made bright pink by combining half green cabbage and half purple.

Ingredients:
1 head cabbage, green or purple
2 tablespoons sea salt, course is fine

2 quart-sized large mouth mason jars
Food processor or knife
Cup or cylinder that fits inside the mason jar, to smash sauerkraut

Directions:
Remove and discard outer leaves of the cabbage, until you get to the clean unblemished leaves underneath. Cut cabbage in half and core. Shred cabbage in food processor using a 'slicing' disk or with a knife, creating thin strips of cabbage. Pack into jars, and add 1 tablespoon salt to each jar. Cover and shake to distribute the salt. Allow to sit out for an hour, until the cabbage wilts. Smash to release juices. Cover again, and allow to ferment on counter for 3 days before transferring to the fridge to store. Sauerkraut is ready to eat after the countertop fermentation.

Homemade Pickles

Ingredients:
A dozen or so small pickling cucumbers, or 3 large cucumbers cut into spears.
2 teaspoons unrefined sea salt per jar
1 teaspoon whey per jar (optional) [page 59]
2 teaspoons mustard seed
2 teaspoons dried dill or 1 tablespoon fresh
Filtered water

Optional: Juice from an already successful lacto fermented vegetable, such as sauerkraut. This helps the ferment to get started faster.

Directions:
Wash cucumbers. The small cucumbers can stay whole. Pack cucumbers into half gallon or quart sized wide mouth mason jars, as many as you need. The pickles can be packed tightly. Distribute the mustard seed and dill among the jars, add any amount of optional ferment juice to each jar and then fill with filtered water to within 1/2 inch of the top, add 2 teaspoons of sea salt (coarse salt is fine). Screw on an airtight lid. Place in a cool room temperature place to ferment for 3-4 days, testing one jar to see if pickles are sufficiently sour. Move all jars to the fridge; unopened they keep for months, use within a couple weeks after opening.
I find fermenting pickles at a cooler room temperature makes crisper pickles, try the basement or a bottom cupboard.

8 STAPLE FOODS

Staple foods are called for here and there in recipes, homemade versions provide more nutrition and authentic taste.

Chicken stock

Ingredients:
Cooked chicken [page 30]
2 tablespoons apple cider vinegar
Optional: 2 tablespoons thyme, 6 cloves garlic, 1 onion, 1 inch of ginger root, vegetable scraps such as the ends of onions and carrots, core of the cabbage, leaves from celery, etc

Directions:
Using your fingers, remove all the meat from the chicken and set aside for another use. Reserve drippings, skin, and bones. Using a large stock pot or slow cooker, place bones, drippings, and skin in. Break large bones to allow the nutritious marrow to get into the stock.

Fill pot 3/4 full with filtered water, add the apple cider vinegar and any optional herbs and vegetables. Cook on medium-high until bubbling, reduce heat to low and allow to simmer, covered, at least 8 hours. When done, allow to cool then pour stock through a strainer and transfer to mason jars to store in the fridge. To strain, use a mesh strainer over a pitcher-style 4-cup measuring cup.

This makes transferring the stock to the mason jars easier; I do one jar at a time, cleaning out the strainer as needed during the process. The fat will rise to the top of the jars in the fridge, which can be included in soups or used as a fat for cooking. Pick any more meat off the bones that you can after the chicken stock has been removed. Discard the remaining bones and if desired, use a blender to puree skin and soft gelatinous bits left on the bones into the stock or soup.

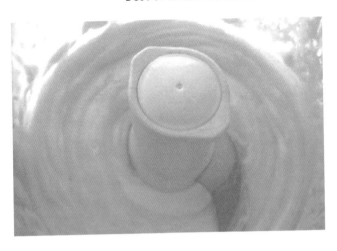

Homemade Mayonnaise

Olive oil makes a more flavorful mayonnaise, and that's what we use. Grapeseed oil has less of a flavor, but the brands of extra virgin grapeseed oil that I've used have been bright green. Once you see how easy and tasty this is, you'll never want to go back to store bought mayo!

Ingredients:
2 raw farm fresh eggs, room temperature
2 cups oil; light olive oil, virgin grape seed oil, or sunflower oil
Pinch of salt
1 tablespoon whey (optional) [page 59]

Directions:
Put the eggs in the food processor or blender, turn on, and take a full minute to pour in each cup of oil, watching a clock with a second hand helps to keep this slow.

By the time two minutes are up (or one minute for one egg/cup of oil) it should be thick! In my experience you have to pour it slowly- dumping it all in at once and then letting it run for a minute doesn't seem to work.
Add a small pinch of sea salt and let it mix in.

Optional: For a probiotic boost, add 1 tablespoon of whey and allow to stand at room temperature for 7 hours to culture before transferring to the fridge.

Store homemade mayonnaise in glass jars with lids. Mayonnaise will thicken in the fridge and is best used within 2 weeks of making it.

Crispy Nuts

Nuts are tasty grain free snacks, but they do contain anti-nutrients (phytic acid) that make them difficult to digest. Soaking in saltwater and then dehydrating eliminates some of the anti-nutrients and makes them taste like a gourmet treat.

To soak nuts:
Place 2-3 lbs raw nuts in a large bowl (they will swell, so only fill 2/3 full, using another bowl if needed). Add 2 tablespoons sea salt and cover the nuts with filtered water. Allow to soak overnight at room temperature (on the counter). No need to cover.

To dry:
Drain in a colander and start dehydrating the nuts you soaked last night, or roast in a pan as low as your oven will go. Dehydrate 12 hours.

Coconut Flour Bread

Using a small loaf pan works best as this doesn't raise much during baking.

Ingredients:
6 eggs
1/3 cup butter, ghee, or coconut oil; soft or melted
1/3 cup applesauce for sweeter bread, or 1 medium onion, pureed, for savory bread
2 tablespoons honey
1/2 teaspoon sea salt
3/4 cup coconut flour

Instructions:
Grease 1 standard sized loaf pan or 2 mini loaf pans well with butter, ghee, or coconut oil. Mix all ingredients until there are no lumps. Pour the batter into bread pan, filling 3/4 full if dividing between multiple mini bread pans. Bake in preheated oven at 350 degrees for 40 minutes for a standard sized loaf, or 25 minutes for mini loaves. Cooking time may vary as loaf pans vary in size; bread is done when a knife inserted into the middle comes out clean. Allow to cool before trying to remove bread from pan. To remove, gently run a butter knife around the outside edges, between the bread and the pan. Flip the bread pan over a plate and (hopefully) it will come out all in one piece. Turn right side up, slice as desired, and store, covered, in the fridge.

Baked Squash

Squash is a lovely side dish on its own and is used in many recipes.

Rinse one baking pumpkin, acorn squash, butternut squash, or any other kind of winter squash. Cut in half. Scoop out seeds and bake cut-side down on a baking sheet or glass baking dish for 1 hour, then turn off the oven and allow to continue baking as the oven cools. Scoop out flesh and freeze in 1-cup increments for use in recipes, or eat as a side dish topped with butter and sea salt or honey.

Roasted squash seeds

Seeds of 1+ squash
1-2 tablespoons coconut oil
½-1 teaspoon sea salt

Scoop the squash seeds out of the squash. Clean the stringy pulp from them, and just add the seeds to 1-2 tablespoons of coconut or palm oil. Spread in a single layer in a dish or pie plate (the same dish you cooked the squash fries in is just fine) and sprinkle with a pinch or sea salt. Bake at 300 degrees for 10-15 minutes until golden brown, stirring once during baking.

SOURCING HIGH QUALITY FOOD

Being able to utilize high quality ingredients is the best part of cooking from scratch. This section describes where to find high quality ingredients used in grain free cooking.

Meat

Meat from sustainably raised animals provides healthy much needed protein in the grain free diet. Finding a local source of beef is the best for the environment, your local economy, and gives you a good sense of knowing your community and where your food comes from. Sometimes you can find local sources of meat by seeing where your local health food stores purchase their meat and then directly contact the source to purchase in bulk. Sustainably raised grassfed meat can also be found online at healthhomehappy.com/meat

Fish and Seafood

Fresh fish can be found at the supermarket or caught on a weekend outing. If purchasing, look to make sure it is *wild caught* and not farmed. We often purchase wild caught salmon and sardines in cans, just look for cans that are BPA free. High quality wild caught salmon, fish, and fish roe can be found online at healthhomehappy.com/seafood

Eggs

The best quality eggs are often sold from farmhouses, not grocery stores. Go check out any signs along country roads that advertise 'farm fresh eggs' and choose eggs from chickens who are busy hunting and in the open air. In the grocery store (what we have to resort to in the wintertime) choose hormone and antibiotic free eggs, organic if possible.

Milk

Raw milk from healthy cows feeding on grass can be found through realmilk.com or your local chapter of the Weston Price Foundation. Unhomogenized organic is the next best choice and is found in your health food store. If you have to drive far to purchase your milk, it can be purchased in bulk and stored in a chest freezer, just pour a cup out to allow for expansion.

Yogurt and kefir cultures: High quality yogurt from the health food store can be used as a yogurt starter. Kefir grains have to be purchased or found locally. For online sources see healthhomehappy.com/kefir

Cheese: Grassfed organic cheese is available online at healthhomehappy.com/cheese Kerrygold cheese is available at most Costco, Trader Joes, and health food stores and this is what we usually buy. Organic goat cheese, or fresh cheese at farmers markets are good choices as well.

Ghee and Butter: Kerrygold butter, Anchor, and Organic Valley are all available in most areas and are high quality. Grassfed ghee can be found at healthhomehappy.com/ghee You may be able to purchase good quality butter from the same place you purchase raw milk.

Almond flour

Almond flour can be found at some health food stores and online at healthhomehappy.com/almondflour

Whole nuts

Whole nuts can be found at health food stores (check the bulk section), Costco, and ordered online at Azurestandard.com. I purchase my almonds from Azure, because conventionally grown almonds (even if they are labeled 'raw') are often pasteurized with a carcinogen. Other than almonds, I do not always purchase organic nuts.

Coconut

Coconut is used a lot in grain free baking. Coconut milk can be purchased less expensively by the case at healthhomehappy.com/coconutmilk Coconut oil, flour, and shredded coconut can be found at healthhomehappy.com/coconut or also in your health food store's bulk food section. Watch for added sugar and preservatives. Coconut flour in this book has been tested with Tropical Traditions brand, coconut flour consistencies can vary considerably, which will affect how recipes turn out.

Produce

Produce can be purchased at farmer's markets, community sustain agriculture co-ops (CSAs), directly from the farm, and from health food or even general grocery stores. Purchasing local fresh produce is always preferred, but for convenience and cost savings grocery store produce is still great to include in your diet.

Herbs and Spices

Organic herbs and spices are found in the bulk section of health food stores and online at healthhomehappy.com/herbs
Some must haves: Sea salt, black pepper, basil, dill, cumin, paprika, thyme, nutmeg, cinnamon, ginger powder, clove powder.

RECOMMENDED KITCHEN EQUIPMENT

I found that I use different kitchen equipment for following a grain free diet than I did with a diet based on grains. Here are some things that I have found useful. Purchase most here: healthhomehappy.com/equipment

Stock pot, stainless steel, 8-10 quart
Sauce pan, stainless steel, 2-1/2 to 3 quart
Skillet, stainless steel with clear glass lid, 10-12 inches
Griddle, cast iron, to fit over two burners
Mason jars, wide mouth; half gallon, quart, and pint
Thermos, wide mouth (good quality pays here)
Dehydrator, Excalibur, 5 tray is big enough for most people; it can be used for fruits and veggies, yogurt, and jerky. Quart jars fit in the 5-tray model.
Food processor, Quisenart or Kitchenaid brand, 9 cup. This machine gets a workout with grain free cooking, use for shredding veggies, making mayonnaise, blending baked goods, grating cheese, and more.
Blender, glass. I use just a simple blender for smoothies and occsional mixing. I prefer to invest in a higher quality food processor and get a basic blender.
Glass {or plastic} lidded storage containers for food on the go
Muffin pan, stoneware, made in the USA
Lofa pan, stoneware or glass, made in the USA
Baking sheet, stainless steel or stoneware
Blender, immersion to puree soups right in the pot.
Water filter, chlorine and fluoride filters for drinking and cooking
Shower filter, chlorine filter

Index

ABOUT THE AUTHOR

Cara lives in Arizona with her two young children. They enjoy the sunshine, swimming, fun day trips (with food packed to bring along!) and hanging out with family.

She believes that natural, sustainably produced and traditionally prepared food is designed by God to be best for the earth and people alike and enjoys learning more about this all the time. Her daughter, Hannah, has been grain free for over two years, and the whole family eats primarily grain free home.

Cara blogs at Health, Home, and Happiness (healthhomehappy.com) about incorporating traditional food, natural remedies, and healthy habits into real life. The goal of her writing is to encourage the average family that eating real wholesome foods is something that is a priority and can realistically be done.

Made in the USA
Lexington, KY
05 May 2012